# LET'S SING ABOUT ANIMALS

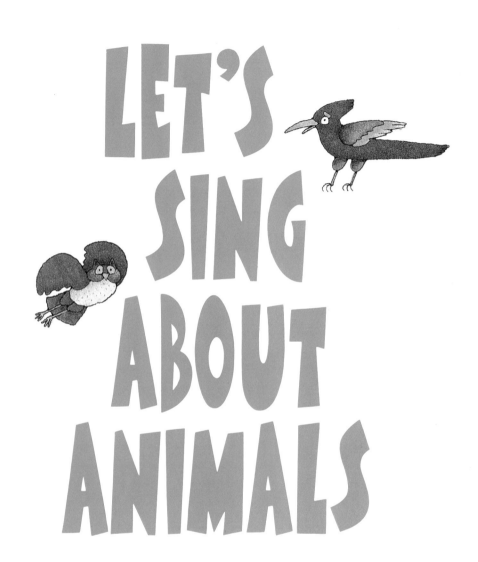

Illustrated by
## Pat Hoggan

**Troll Associates**

LIBRARY OF CONGRESS CATALOGING-IN-PUBLICATION DATA
Let's sing about animals / illustrated by Pat Hoggan.
p. of music. — (Troll singalongs)
For voice and piano, with chord symbols.
Words and music of 2 songs by George James, the remainder arranged
by James.
Summary: A collection of songs about animals, including "Eensy
Weensy Spider," "Unicorn," and "Five Little Monkeys."
ISBN 0-8167-2980-8 (lib. bdg.)      ISBN 0-8167-2981-6 (pbk.)
1. Children's songs.    2. Animals—Songs and music—Juvenile.
[1. Animals—Songs and music.    2. Songs.]    I. Hoggan, Pat, ill.
II. James, George.    III. Series.
M1997.L583   1993                              92-763080

Published by Troll Associates
Words and music for "Animals" and "Animal March" by George James
Original arrangements for all other titles by George James
Text copyright © 1993 Troll Associates
Illustration copyright © 1993 Pat Hoggan
The publisher wishes to thank Randa Kirshbaum for her transcriptions
of these original musical arrangements.

Printed in the United States of America
10  9  8  7  6  5  4  3  2  1

# Contents

# Animals

Words and music by George James

*Relaxed*

Chorus

An-i-mals,  an-i-mals,  let's all talk a-bout  an-i-mals.

An-i-mals,  an-i-mals,  let's all sing a-bout  an-i-mals. Some

growl,  some bark,  some go walk-ing  in  a  park.  There are

those  who wait 'til dark  to say,  "Who?  Yes, you."  Some

laugh,  some sing.  Some don't  sound like  an - y - thing.  Some make

D♭                                    A♭7

lots   of   noise        like it's    a   hol- i- day.                              That they're

*Chorus*

2. Some quack, some squeak,
   some are quiet when they speak.
   There are those who trumpet, get out of the way.
   They're big, they're small,
   some are short, some are tall,
   but whatever they are,
   it's safe for us to say that they're …

*Chorus*

# The Fox

Arranged by George James

*Lively*

The fox went out— on a chill-y night. He prayed for the moon to

give him light, for he'd man-y a mile to go that night be -

fore he'd reach the town - o, town - o, town- o,—

man-y a mile to go that night be - fore he'd reach the town - o.

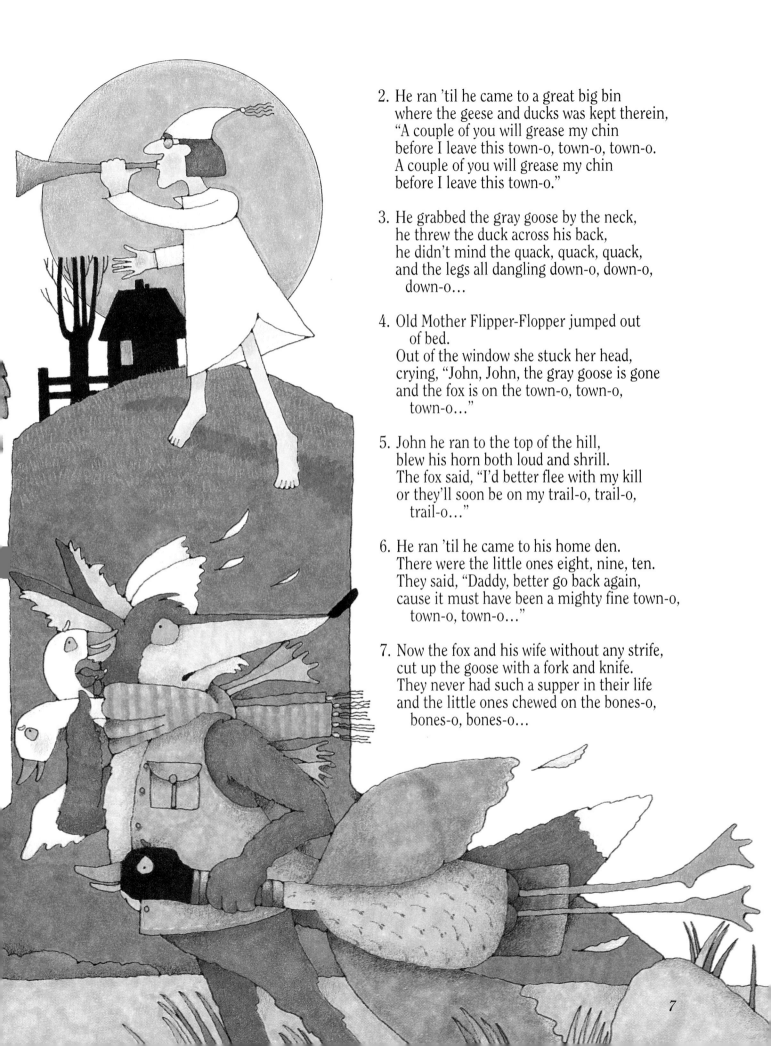

2. He ran 'til he came to a great big bin
   where the geese and ducks was kept therein,
   "A couple of you will grease my chin
   before I leave this town-o, town-o, town-o.
   A couple of you will grease my chin
   before I leave this town-o."

3. He grabbed the gray goose by the neck,
   he threw the duck across his back,
   he didn't mind the quack, quack, quack,
   and the legs all dangling down-o, down-o,
   down-o…

4. Old Mother Flipper-Flopper jumped out
   of bed.
   Out of the window she stuck her head,
   crying, "John, John, the gray goose is gone
   and the fox is on the town-o, town-o,
   town-o…"

5. John he ran to the top of the hill,
   blew his horn both loud and shrill.
   The fox said, "I'd better flee with my kill
   or they'll soon be on my trail-o, trail-o,
   trail-o…"

6. He ran 'til he came to his home den.
   There were the little ones eight, nine, ten.
   They said, "Daddy, better go back again,
   cause it must have been a mighty fine town-o,
   town-o, town-o…"

7. Now the fox and his wife without any strife,
   cut up the goose with a fork and knife.
   They never had such a supper in their life
   and the little ones chewed on the bones-o,
   bones-o, bones-o…

7

# Eensy Weensy Spider

Arranged by George James

The een - sy ween - sy spi - der climbed up the wa - ter spout.

Down came the rain and washed the spi - der out.

Out came the sun and dried up all the rain, and the

een - sy ween - sy spi - der climbed up the spout a - gain.

Spi - der, spi - der, een - sy ween - sy spi - der.

# I Had A Little Rooster

Arranged by George James

2. I had a little hen by the barnyard gate
   and that little hen was my playmate,
   and that little hen said, "Chick, chick, chick,"
   and that little rooster said, "Cock-a-doodle-doo,
   doo, doo, doo, doo, doo, doo, doo, doo, doo, doo."

3. I had a little duck …   "Quack, quack, quack,"
   and that little hen said …
   and that little rooster said …

4. I had a little pig …   "Oink, oink, oink,"
   and that little duck said …
   and that little hen said …
   and that little rooster said …

11

# A Fly Walked In

Arranged by George James

A fly walked in-to a gro - cery store, a - lone, all a -

lone. He'd nev - er been in a store be - fore, a - lone, all a -

lone. He walked on the bread, put his feet on the jam, and

stuck out his tongue at the gro - cery man, and then he walked out of the

store a - gain, a - lone, all a - lone.

2. A fly walked into the barber shop,
   alone, all alone.
For a haircut he did stop,
   alone, all alone.
He walked on the comb, put his feet
   on the chair,
as the barber said, "You don't have any hair."
The fly he walked right out of there,
alone, all alone.

3. A fly walked into the butcher's store,
   alone, all alone.
He slipped all around on the sawdust floor,
   alone, all alone.
He sat on the ham, put his feet on the chop.
The butcher thought he would never stop.
Then out of there he decided to hop,
   alone, all alone.

13

# Unicorn

Arranged by George James

un — i - corn?

2. In another part of the lonely wood
   a cyclops prowled up to no good.
   His one eye peered from the middle of
      his head.
   He was hungry and it was time to be fed.

3. He saw the unicorn standing there
   and silently crept out from his lair,
   when suddenly to his great surprise
   the unicorn looked up with fearful eyes.

*Chorus*

4. The cyclops froze right where he stood
   and love found its way into that dark wood.
   The unicorn flashed a mysterious smile
   and a tear fell from the cyclops' only eye.

5. "Ah-ha, my friend," the unicorn said,
   "why is that eye in the middle of your head?
   Rather than see you so forlorn
   I'd gladly give up my only horn."

6. Then a flash of light never seen since
   and the cyclops turned into a two-eyed
      prince.
   The unicorn without his horn, of course,
   became the prince's favorite horse.

*Chorus*

# Kookaburra

Arranged by George James

2. Kookaburra, he's such a royal bird.
   Kookaburra, it's such a funny word.
   Laugh, kookaburra, laugh, kookaburra,
   happy as can be.

3. Kookaburra sits in the old gum tree
   eating all the gumdrops he can see.
   Stop, kookaburra, stop, kookaburra,
   leave some there for me.

*Repeat last line.*

*Repeat last line of verse 1, twice.*

17

# A Froggy Went A-Courtin'

Arranged by George James

Country style

A frog-gy went a-court-in' and he did ride, uh, huh.

A frog-gy went a-court-in' and he did ride, uh,

huh! A frog-gy went a-court-in' and

he did ride— with a sword and pis - tol by his side, uh,—

huh. Uh, huh!

2. He rode up to Miss Mousie's door, uh, huh!
He rode up to Miss Mousie's door, uh, huh!
He rode up to Miss Mousie's door,
and he knocked so hard that his fist got sore, uh, huh! Uh, huh!

3. He took Miss Mousie on his knee, uh, huh!…
and he said, "Miss Mousie, will you marry me, uh, huh! Uh, huh!"

4. Miss Mousie said, "I'm filled with pride, uh, huh!"…
and I will be your happy bride, uh, huh! Uh, huh!"

5. Oh, where will the wedding supper be, uh, huh?…
Way down yonder in a hollow tree, uh, huh! Uh, huh!

6. Now, the first to come was a little white moth, uh, huh!…
Around her neck was a tablecloth, uh, huh! Uh, huh!

7. The next to come was an old red hen, uh, huh!…
She played a little tune and she played it again, uh, huh! Uh, huh!

8. Next to come was a nice brown cow, uh, huh!…
She tried to dance but she didn't know how, uh, huh! Uh, huh!

9. They all gathered 'round the lucky pair, uh, huh!…
Singing and dancing everywhere, uh, huh! Uh, huh!

# I Had A Little Dog

*Walking song*

Arranged by George James

had a lit-tle dog and his name was Paul._____ *(Whistle or hum)*

gave him a lit-tle but he want-ed it all._____ *(Whistle or hum)*

*fine*

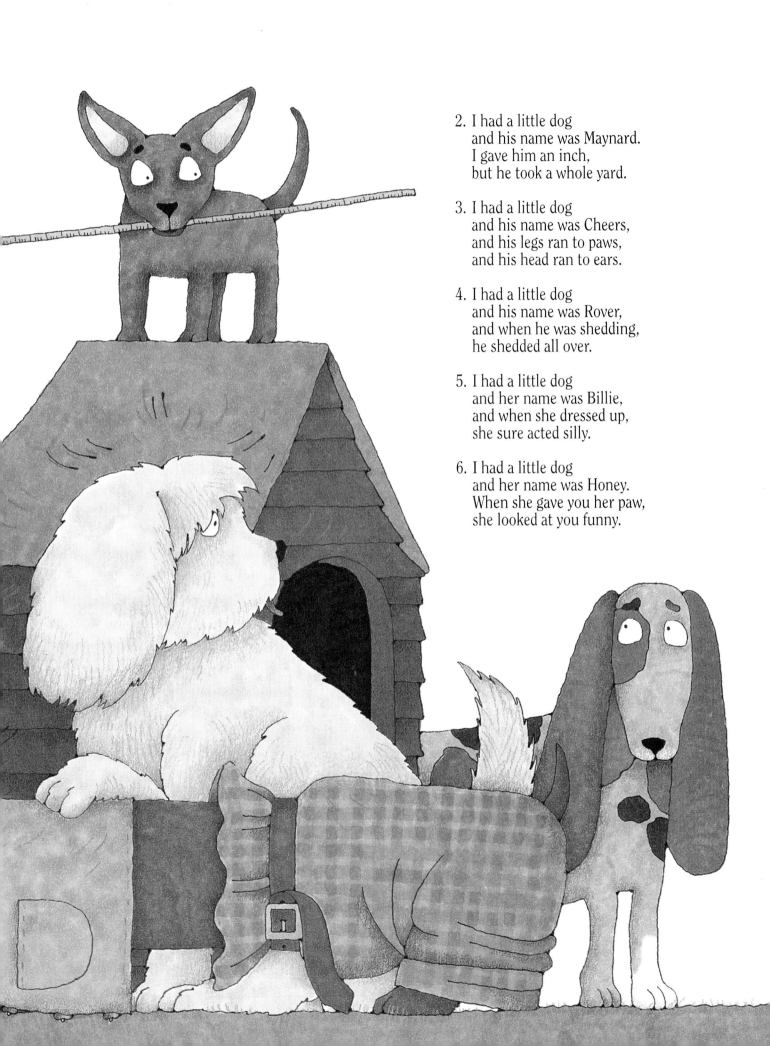

2. I had a little dog
   and his name was Maynard.
   I gave him an inch,
   but he took a whole yard.

3. I had a little dog
   and his name was Cheers,
   and his legs ran to paws,
   and his head ran to ears.

4. I had a little dog
   and his name was Rover,
   and when he was shedding,
   he shedded all over.

5. I had a little dog
   and her name was Billie,
   and when she dressed up,
   she sure acted silly.

6. I had a little dog
   and her name was Honey.
   When she gave you her paw,
   she looked at you funny.

# I Wish

Arranged by George James

2. I wish I were a squirrel so fat,
   a real good squirrel I'd be,
   and just before the sun went down,
   I'd climb up the old oak,...
   climb up the old oak tree.

3. I wish I were a pig in the dirt,
   a real good pig I'd be,
   and just before the sun went down,
   I'd sit by the old oak,...sit by the old oak tree.

4. And if I were a mole in the ground,
   a real good mole I'd be.
   You'd find me when the sun went down,
   under the old oak,...under the
   old oak tree.

# Animal March

Arranged by George James

Al - li - ga - tor, hedge-hog, ant - eat - er, bear, rat - tle- snake, buf-fa - lo, an - a - con - da, hare.

2. Bullfrog, woodchuck, wolverine, goose,
   whippoorwill, chipmunk, jackal, moose.

3. Mud turtle, whale, glowworm, bat,
   salamander, snail, and a Maltese cat.

4. Black squirrel, fox, opossum, wren,
   red squirrel, loon, and a prairie hen.

5. Polecat, dog, wild otter, rat,
   pelican, hog, dodo, and bat.

6. Eagle, kangaroo, sheep, duck, and widgeon,
   conger, armadillo, beaver, seal, pigeon.

7. Reindeer, black snake, ibex, nightingale,
   martin, wild drake, crocodile, and quail.

8. House rat, toe rat, white bear, doe,
   chickadee, peacock, bobolink, and crow.

# Boa Constrictor

*Chorus*

2. Make haste, he's got my waist.
   Be calm, he's got my arm.
   That's grand, he's got my hand.
   That bum, he's got my thumb.

*Chorus*

3. Oh, yes, he's got my chest.
   Oh, heck, he's got my neck.
   Hey, Ted, he's got my head.
   I said, Ted, he's got my head!

# Five Little Monkeys

Arranged by George James

*Fast*

Five lit-tle mon—keys jump-in' on the bed, one fell off and bumped his head. Ma-ma called the doc - tor and the doc-tor said, "No more mon-key bus' - ness jump-in' on the bed."

2. Four little monkeys jumpin' on the bed,
   one fell off and bumped his head.
   Mama called the doctor and the doctor said,
   "No more monkey bus'ness jumpin' on the bed."

3. Three little monkeys …

4. Two little monkeys …

5. One little monkey …

6. No more monkeys jumpin' on the bed,
   no more monkeys bumpin' their head.
   No more calling doctors, and doctors no more said,
   "No more monkey bus'ness jumpin' on the bed."

# Tailor And The Mouse

Ram - sey, hi - did-dle un - kum o - ver the sea, hi - did-dle un - kum fid-dle dee dee.

2. The tailor had a tall silk hat,
   Hi-diddle unkum feedle.
   The mouse he ate it, fancy that!
   Hi-diddle unkum feedle.

*Chorus*

3. The tailor thought the mouse was ill,…
   He gave him part of a big blue pill,…

*Chorus*

4. The tailor thought the mouse would die,…
   So he baked him up an apple pie,…

*Chorus*

5. The mouse he ate it and got all better,…
   He sent the tailor a thank-you letter,…

*Chorus*